OCD Relief Now!

Boris Pisman, LMHC

ISBN-10: 0615558739
ISBN-13:978-0615558738

DEDICATION

To all OCD Sufferers and their Families. May you discover peace while living with OCD.

ACKNOWLEDGMENTS

Thanks goes Swami Satchidanandaji and J. Krishnamurti. Also, thanks goes to all non-duality teachers I have read or studied with.

CONTENTS

HOW TO USE THIS BOOK

It is simple. Read the first three chapters. You will need to practice them for a few weeks, but do not wait too long. Begin to apply these practices to your OCD as soon as possible. The idea is to incorporate these first three chapters into your work on your OCD. When you find yourself obsessing, refer to the chapter devoted to the type of OCD applicable to you right now. These chapters start with a real example of a person suffering from OCD, then describe obsessions you may be experiencing at any given time and then advise you on what to do or not to do right in the moment. OCD Relief Now! is your constant companion for those times when you find yourself obsessing and feeling anxious. This guide is like having a trained OCD coach with you all the time.

HOW TO STAY RELAXED

Relaxation alone will not cure your OCD. If you see a therapist who teaches you how to relax and does nothing else, you may want to consider finding a new therapist. Yet focusing primarily on analyzing your obsessions sometimes seems to lead to more obsessions and anxiety. Combining treatment with relaxation can improve your results.

Knowing how to stay relaxed while obsessing and feeling anxious is an important part of your recovery. Staying relaxed will help you to face fearful obsessions and feelings more productively. Relaxation will assist you in your recovery from OCD. Relaxation is easy if you know how to do it and what it means.

Often, your loved ones will tell you to "relax and let it go." Some of you find it insulting and demeaning. If you could do it, you would. From the point of view of yoga, to relax is to release tension from the body. Due to external and internal stress, you can lose the ability to stay relaxed. You walk around in a constant "fight or flight" mode. It is exhausting for your nervous system and your mental health. To change this pattern, start slowly – begin to learn how to stay relaxed. It takes a few weeks of formal practice to become familiar with this technique. Then it needs to be applied to your stressful situations on a daily basis.

The practice consists of lying on the floor, or on a bed, and telling each part of the body to relax. You are using your mental powers in order to relax your body. You are retraining your body to stay relaxed. All you do is give a mental command to each different part of the body to relax.

Here is the formal practice itself. Please practice the following method over the course of a few weeks: Lay on a flat surface, have your arms alongside your body, and your palms up. Your legs should be shoulder distance apart. Your chin is slightly tucked in. Eyes are closed. Do not rush. This practice should take around 10 or 15 minutes. Visualize different parts of your body. All you have to do is to give a mental command to each part of the body – that is all there is to it.

Tell your feet to relax; tell your ankles to relax; tell your knees to relax; tell your thighs to relax. Relax your pelvis, abdomen, chest, upper chest and ribcage. Tell your heart, lungs and abdominal organs to relax. Relax your lower back, middle back and upper back. Tell your fingers and palms to relax; relax your wrists, forearms, elbows, upper arms and shoulders. Tell your neck to relax, jaw, lips, tongue, facial muscles, eyes, ears, forehead, back of the head and top of the head. Mentally see your body on the floor or bed being completely relaxed.

Now take five minutes or so to feel and enjoy the gentle pull of gravity. Do nothing. If you notice that a part of your body gets tense again, all you have to do is tell it to relax. Do not expect perfection; just continue monitoring your body for tension.

Now you know how to work to relieve your tension. Often when you obsess and feel anxious, you do not notice how tense your body becomes. It is better to try to stay relaxed and obsess, than to obsess and be tense. Begin to take charge of your OCD – even if you cannot stop obsessing or, when you are being compulsive, at least stay relaxed. Simply scan your body for tension during anxiety and tell the part of the body that is tense to relax. You can do it sitting at a desk, talking to someone, riding in a car or anytime at all.

Your effort to stay relaxed should not be done obsessively. Simply do the relaxation practice when you find yourself feeling anxious. Come back to scanning your body for tension when you remember to do it. As you continue doing it, you will learn to keep the body free from tension even though you may be obsessing and feeling anxious. Combine this practice with your work on OCD, including patience and acceptance.

WHAT TO DO WITH YOUR BREATH

Notice how you breathe when you are feeling anxious or having an obsession. Is your breath shallow? Do you breathe with your upper chest? Are your abdominal muscles tight? Make yourself aware of your breathing. The way you breathe can make a difference between having a panic attack and just being anxious.

It is hard to face your obsessions and compulsions when you are having a panic attack. As you work on your obsessions and compulsions, the way you breathe can either make them tolerable or make you feel more anxious. To be able to handle and manage your OCD means learning to desensitize your nervous system to scary thoughts, ideas and images. Knowing how to breathe will make it easier to stay calm and relaxed when you obsess or feel anxious.

There are a number of breathing exercises that calm your nervous system. In yoga they are called Pranayama. Although all breathing exercises may be helpful if you practice them on regular basis, abdominal breathing is the most import technique or way of breathing for you to learn to use when you obsess or become compulsive.

Some of you may already know how to do it. If you do, please remember to breathe diaphragmatically when you feel anxious. Simply check to see if your belly gently moves in when you exhale and out when you inhale. If you notice that you are breathing with the chest or upper chest, please bring the breathing lower, toward your belly. This alone will relax your abdominal muscles and lower the stress. Breathing diaphragmatically reduces your anxiety and triggers the sympathetic nervous system, which is in charge of the relaxation response.

If you do not know how to breathe diaphragmatically, it will take a few weeks of practice to get comfortable. To learn how to do it, please lay down on the floor or a bed, put a book or a pillow on your belly and, as you inhale, gently push your belly up allowing air to move into the lower part of your lungs. As you exhale, gently pull your belly in, expelling air from your lungs. To repeat, as you inhale, let the belly go up, pushing the book or pillow up and, as you exhale, let the book or pillow go down. Once you practice this for five to ten minutes a day for two weeks, you will know how to breathe diaphragmatically.

You may also practice diaphragmatic breathing sitting up or standing up. Simply put your right or left palm on your belly making sure that your belly goes out as you inhale and moves gently in as you exhale. During the day, occasionally check to see if you are breathing diaphragmatically. This is a good way to keep stress down and a very helpful way to help you learn how to deal with your obsessions, compulsions and anxiety. Please remember to apply this when you obsess or are feeling anxious.

MEDITATION FOR OCD AND ANXIETY

Do not think that if you do not meditate, you will not be able to overcome your OCD. Meditation is not magic. Most types of meditation practiced in the United States are simply techniques learned from meditation teachers. There are many meditation techniques. Most of them teach you to focus on something like a word (mantra), breath, third eye, sound, energy center (chakra), or symbol, or to observe your thoughts, emotions and sensations.

To meditate is to sit in a quiet place, in a comfortable position, with your eyes open or closed and to put your mental effort into concentrating on something or observing without paying too much attention to passing thoughts and images. As soon as you become aware that you got distracted, you should bring your attention back to concentrating or observing.

Many people give up meditation because they feel frustrated that they cannot do it, or they actually get more angry, anxious or emotional during or after meditation. It seems that some people feel that meditation is not for them. Meditate if you want to, but try to understand that using your will power in meditation is counterproductive. Forcing yourself to meditate, concentrate or observe will not create calmness and peace. Intense concentration or observation will result in frustration, feeling helpless and perhaps in a headache.

If you chose to meditate, notice if you are avoiding your thoughts and emotions during meditation. Refocusing on the object of meditation or observation may act as an escape from feeling anxious or being scared of thoughts, images and ideas. If you have OCD, your meditation should be much simpler. Your meditation should be to sit comfortably with eyes open or closed and let every thought, emotion, feeling, image and idea remain as is. Nothing needs to be changed. Do not make yourself focus or observe; awareness is your natural state minus your thoughts. Awareness expands as you learn how not to engage your thoughts and emotions. Meditation should be effortless and pleasant. Yes, occasionally you will feel stressed and anxious while meditating, so use this practice as your own personal lab — you will eventually have to take your experience out into the real world. It is a waste of time to spend time in meditation avoiding thoughts and emotions. Do not do it.

To summarize, please sit comfortably with your eyes closed or open and let every thought, idea, image and emotion remain as it is. Nothing has to be done. Stay effortless and stay relaxed. Allow your mind to be free. Notice if you feel scared by permitting your mind to be free. Notice your judgments – they are just thoughts. Everything stays as is. Meditation will become more pleasant as you practice it. Your awareness will expand to embrace disturbing obsessions and anxiety. Meditate 10 minutes a day as a formal practice.

HOARDING

Angela is an Ivy League college-educated professional. She is a comptroller at a large company, owns a beautiful two-bedroom condominium in New York City, enjoys the company of a lovely cat and has a number of good friends. She is smart and has a good sense of humor.

She is very embarrassed about the state of her apartment. The bedrooms, closets and living room are full of stuff that she feels she will need one day or that has some kind of sentimental value. Angela sleeps in her living room since her bedrooms are so full they are no longer available for their intended use. She has problems paying her personal bills not because of lack of money, but because she feels overwhelmed. She has difficulties going through her mail for fear of throwing out something important and she gets angry when someone offers to help her clean her apartment. Angela thinks she is missing out on life.

People who hoard things or information often think the following:

I need it. I will use it someday. It has sentimental meaning to me. It belonged to my mother, father, children, etc. I will use it for my work. I find it overwhelming to go through my stuff and deal with it. It may be useful to me one day. I need to have more than one because it could be difficult to get another one. I need to recycle it because I am an environmentally conscious person. I must know this to impress others or to learn.

What to do and/or not do (Please read many times while obsessing and practice what is said):

These thoughts are not unique to you. They are universal to all Hoarders. Your OCD creates doubt, needs certainty and requires perfection. This type of thinking is normal to all people suffering from Obsessive Compulsive Disorder. Understanding these qualities of OCD will help you to overcome it. If your house or apartment is full of stuff, if you are embarrassed to invite guests to your home, if your relatives or landlord or a judge think you have a problem with Hoarding, it is time to deal with it. Remember that you will experience anxiety and anger while working on this disorder, but you must acquire the skill to get rid of things. It takes time to master this skill, but it is possible.

Do not give much credence to your feelings of anxiety or anger. They are normal when you are working on your problem and, as time passes, you will not experience them as much. Hoarding Thoughts will lead you to have more stuff; hence, the OCD-affected part of your mind is not telling you the truth. Simply become aware of Hoarding Thoughts and see them as a product of your OCD and not as reality. Reality did not put you in this situation – your disorder did! In other words, begin to distrust these thoughts. You've spent your lifetime trusting Hoarding Thoughts, so it is time to try something else. To distrust your Hoarding Thoughts means to see that not everything your mind tells you is beneficial. If your thinking leads to Hoarding, it is your OCD that is the problem.

Your life is limited because of OCD. Understand that your mind has been giving you wrong information regarding the importance of the stuff you have accumulated. It is time to stop validating these thoughts. You stop validating an obsession when you are no longer engaged in it. Not to engage with an obsession means not to have a conversation with it in your mind. As you argue with a thought or try to reassure yourself or agree with an obsession, you create an internal conflict. This conflict must be eliminated for an obsession to pass. By not engaging with the obsession, you deprive it of the energy generated by the conflict and you allow the obsession to pass. When you engage your obsessions, you are back in the disorder.

In order not to engage an obsession, your attention has to be somewhere else. Your brain has a natural capacity to observe and be aware of thoughts. To be aware of your obsession means not to judge it or make conclusions about yourself based on this obsession. To be aware is to be in a space free from thinking. To observe is not to think. It is as if thinking is happening, but judgment is not there. When you catch yourself judging, realize that judging is just another form of thinking.

To be aware is to create space for thoughts to arise, exist and dissipate. To be aware is to observe your emotions of anger, fear and uncertainty and allow them to exist until they dissipate. To be aware is to step aside and let the obsession pass. To be aware is to learn to react less. To be aware is to see that an obsession expressed as a thought, an image or an urge is just another thought and that thoughts pass if you let them be and do nothing about them. To be aware is to realize that not wanting to have an obsession is to have just another thought. To be aware is to let things be as they are. As you learn not to react to anxious thoughts, your nervous system gets stronger. In order for you to successfully manage your OCD, choose to connect to your awareness – it is a quiet and peaceful place.

When anxiety or anger increases, remind yourself that you are suffering from OCD and that is why you are feeling these emotions. Once you realize and practice distrusting your Hoarding obsession, you can start by not bringing stuff home. As you succeed in this first step, it is time to spend 20 to 30 minutes a day getting rid of stuff. Staying in awareness and allowing space for the feeling and obsession to arise, exist and dissipate will make you stronger and prepare you to clear your home or apartment at your own pace.

Summary:

Remember your Hoarding obsession is not unique. All Hoarders think similar thoughts. Your mind is giving you wrong information. Stay in awareness. Do not engage your obsession. Do not validate your feelings. Stop bringing new stuff home. Spend 20 to 30 minutes each day getting rid of stuff and allow space for your emotions and thoughts to arise, exist and dissipate.

CHECKING OCD

Barbara has a Ph.D. in geology. She works for a very famous New York-based organization. She does a lot of research, supervises a number of interns and she is considered one of the most knowledgeable people in her profession. She is kind and considerate.

Barbara takes about an hour to leave her house. She starts with checking her stove, which she almost never uses. Then she unplugs all electrical equipment, checks the kitchen and bathroom faucets and makes sure the windows and doors are closed. She stares at the stove for at least ten to fifteen minutes making sure that all the knobs are off. Often, after Barbara leaves her house, she then comes back to double check. She is terrified she may accidently cause injury or damage to others. This behavior is very frustrating to her.

People who check often think the following:

How do I know I turned it off? It will be my fault if I hurt someone by not being careful. It will be too much for me to replace my documents or things if they get destroyed. It makes sense to be careful. I do not want to hurt anyone by forgetting to turn off or close it. Someone may harm my family and me. It just does not feel right — I should check again. Did I check it? I do not remember.

What to do and/or not do (Please read many times while obsessing and practice what is said):

These thoughts are not unique to you. They are universal to all Checkers. Your OCD creates doubt, needs certainty and requires perfection. This type of thinking is normal to all people suffering from Obsessive Compulsive Disorder. Understanding these qualities of OCD will help you to overcome it. Some people with Checking Obsessions and Compulsions check for 45 minutes, some may do it for 10 minutes. Either way, checking is life limiting, sad and frustrating. Checkers get embarrassed because they are late for appointments, they may lose their jobs or they do not get promotions. People without OCD do not understand people who check and find it frustrating to be with them.

It seems that the more you check, the less confident you feel. In fact, research has proven that it is true. As you stare at something for a long time, you begin to feel unsure if the door is

closed, the stove is off or the car door is locked.
It becomes very hard to walk away. You
continuously doubt that you checked enough.
You trust your OCD and do what it tells you to
do – which is to check again. You experience
anxiety and confusion. You think and feel that it
makes sense to check more – it comes so
naturally to you.

Remember that you will experience anxiety and
doubt while working on your disorder and that it
takes time to start trusting your eyes and your
mind again. As you start cutting down on
Checking, you will feel anxious. You will feel
anxious because of your OCD. Do not give
much credence to your feelings of anxiety. You
are trying something new. Once you learn and
practice how to handle your Checking Obsession,
the anxiety will diminish.

Your life is limited because of OCD. Do not
argue with your obsession. Do not try to reason
with it. If you try to reason with it, it only gets
stronger and confuses you more. Understand
that your mind has been giving you wrong
information. It is time to stop validating these
thoughts. You stop validating obsessions when

you are no longer engaged in them. Not to
engage with an obsession means not to have a
conversation with it in your mind. As you argue
with a thought or try to reassure yourself or agree
with an obsession you create an internal conflict.
This conflict must be eliminated for an obsession
to pass. By not engaging with the obsession, you
deprive it of the energy generated by the conflict
and you allow the obsession to pass. When you
engage your obsessions, you are back in the
disorder.

In order not to engage an obsession, your
attention has to be somewhere else. Your brain
has a natural capacity to observe and be aware of
thoughts. To be aware of your obsession means
not to judge it or make conclusions about
yourself or situations around you. To be aware is
to be in a space free from thinking. To observe
is not to think. It is as if thinking is happening,
but judgment is not there. When you catch
yourself judging, realize that judging is just
another form of thinking.

To be aware is to create space for thoughts to
arise, exist and dissipate. To be aware is to
observe your emotions of fear and uncertainty

and allow them to exist until they dissipate. To be aware is to step aside and let the obsession pass. To be aware is to learn to react less. To be aware is to see that an obsession, an image or an urge is just another thought or feeling. Thoughts and feelings pass if you let them be and do nothing about them. To be aware is to realize that not wanting to have an obsession or approaching it with aversion is to have more thoughts. To be aware is to let things be as they are. As you learn not to react to anxious thoughts, your nervous system gets stronger. In order for you successfully manage your OCD, choose to connect to your awareness – it is a quiet and peaceful place and it is always there.

As you cut down on Checking and try to walk away, your anxiety and uncertainty will increase. Remind yourself that you are suffering from OCD and that is why you are feeling these emotions. Do not argue with scary thoughts. Do not engage them. Let things be as they are. Stay in awareness, allow space for the feeling and obsession to arise, exist and dissipate. It will make you stronger and will let you reduce your Checking time at your own pace because you know it has to be done.

Summary:

Remember that your Checking Obsession is not unique. All Checkers think similar thoughts. You have OCD and that is why you think and feel this way. Practice staying in awareness. Do not engage your obsessions. Let things be as they are. Do not validate your feelings. Stop checking gradually, one thing at a time, one room at a time and allow space for emotions and thoughts to arise, exist and dissipate.

CONTAMINATION OCD

Charlie works as a computer programmer. He is well respected at work. His job is located in the financial district, but he lives uptown. Most days, Charlie walks to work and also walks home. He is not able to take the subway and rarely takes a bus because since childhood he has been afraid of rat poison. (Although the exercise keeps him from gaining weight, he hates it because he has never had a problem with his weight.)

Very few people pay attention to signs in the subway or on buildings stating that the premises have been sprayed with rat poison. Charlie sees rat poison everywhere. His wife divorced him because he insisted that she take her shoes off outside the apartment and wanted her to remove her clothes at the door upon arriving home each night and put them in the washing machine. There were no exceptions; all family members had to do this if they went out.

When he pays me for a session, he puts his money or a check on the desk and then I am allowed to take it. Charlie is afraid that if he and

I touch a check or cash at the same time, I will transmit rat poison to him.

People who obsess about Contamination often think the following:

It does not feel clean. What if I shook his hand and he has HIV? If I touch it and do not wash my hands, I will get brain damage, poisoned, a cold, etc. If I touch urine or feces, or they touch my body, I will get sick. My body does not feel clean. I must wipe the seat before I sit down. The food in this restaurant is not clean. What if someone touched this food? My thoughts are affected by people's energy. My body is affected by people's energy. People's thoughts can affect me. I am too sensitive and not able to protect myself from other people's thoughts or energy.

What to do and/or not do (Please read many times while obsessing and practice what is said):

These thoughts are not unique to you. They are universal to all people suffering from Contamination OCD. Your OCD creates doubt, needs certainty and requires perfectionism. This type of thinking is normal to all people suffering from Obsessive Compulsive Disorder. Seeing these qualities of OCD will help you to overcome it. People with Contamination Obsessions and Compulsions suffer greatly. Some wash their hands until they bleed. Some are not able to work. Some have a hard time shopping, bringing things home or accepting gifts. They tend to isolate themselves, feel embarrassed about their thoughts and worry that other people may think they are crazy. Loved ones tend to question if people with Contamination OCD are sane because it is one of the most visible types of OCD.

You seem to see and feel Contamination everywhere or you think about it most of the time. The only time you may feel relaxed is when you are home, after a long shower, sitting in your comfortable non-contaminated area. Part of you knows that what you do is too much, but you cannot stop. You see potential problems everywhere, so your life is very limited. You want to stop washing or being afraid, but you cannot. Your OCD has you completely under its spell.

Remember that you will experience anxiety and fear while working on treating your obsession and that it takes time to start getting better. As you stop doing compulsions of avoidance, you will feel anxious. You may feel anxiety as you never felt before because you will have to not wash or not avoid things. You do not have to do special exposure because your daily living is your exposure. You will feel anxious because of your OCD. Do not give much credence to your feelings of anxiety. You are trying something new. Once you learn and practice how to stop the compulsions, the anxiety will diminish.

Your life is limited because of OCD. Do not try to calm yourself down. Do not argue with your obsessions. Do not try to reason with them. If you try to reason with them, they only get stronger and scarier. Understand that your mind has been catastrophising or bringing up empty memories. It does not matter that you have gotten sick in the past, or you read somewhere that you can get brain damage from touching and then swallowing something, or you read somewhere how other people's thoughts and emotions may affect you. All of it is now just another obsession, just an empty memory. It is time to stop validating these thoughts. You stop validating obsessions when you are no longer engaged in them. Not to engage with an obsession means not to have a conversation with it in your mind. As you argue with a thought or try to reassure yourself or agree with an obsession you create an internal conflict. This conflict must be eliminated for an obsession to pass. By not engaging with the obsession, you deprive it of the energy generated by the conflict and you allow the obsession to pass. When you engage your obsessions, you are back in the disorder.

In order not to engage an obsession, your attention has to be somewhere else. Your brain has a natural capacity to observe and be aware of thoughts. To be aware of your obsessions means not to judge them or make conclusions about yourself or situations around you. To be aware is to be in a space free from thinking. To observe is not to think. It is as if thinking is happening, but judgment is not there. When you catch yourself judging, realize that judging is just another form of thinking.

To be aware is to create space for thoughts to arise, exist and dissipate. To be aware is to observe your emotions of fear and uncertainty and allow them to exist until they dissipate. To be aware is to step aside and let the obsession pass. To be aware is to learn to react less. To be aware is to see that an obsession, an image or an urge is just another thought or feeling. Thoughts and feelings pass if you let them be and do nothing about them. To be aware is to realize that not wanting to have an obsession or approaching it with aversion is to have more thoughts. To be aware is to let things be as they are. As you learn not to react to anxious thoughts, your nervous system gets stronger. In order for you to successfully manage your OCD, choose to connect to your awareness – it is a quiet and peaceful place and it is always there.

As you cut down on washing and avoidance, your anxiety and uncertainty will increase. Remind yourself that you are suffering from OCD and that is why you are feeling these emotions. Do not argue with scary thoughts. Do not engage them. Let things be as they are. Stay in awareness, allow space for the feeling and obsession to arise, exist and dissipate. It will make you stronger and will let you reduce your washing time at your own pace because you know this has to be done.

Summary:

Remember that your Contamination Obsessions
are not unique. All people with Contamination
Obsessions think similar thoughts. You have
OCD and that is why you think and feel this way.
Practice staying in awareness when you have the
urge to wash or to avoid. Do not engage your
obsessions. Let things be as they are. Do not
validate your feelings. Gradually stop washing or
avoiding. Cut the time you wash or stop
avoiding mental or energetic contamination and
allow space for emotions and thoughts to arise,
exist and dissipate.

RELIGIOUS SCRUPULOSITY

David enjoys reading the Bible. He believes that the Bible is the word of God. He and his family prefer to learn directly from the Bible without what they call "intermediaries" such as priests or religious figures. To him and his family, the Bible is the ultimate source of knowledge. They get together to read and pray.

Unfortunately, David suffers from OCD. He is a very lively and intelligent young man who easily dispenses advice to other, but when it comes to the Bible, he often finds himself in conflict. He goes back and forth between the Old and New Testaments. It seems that the Old and New Testaments occasionally contradict each other. David is not able to decide which one is the right one since both, according to David, were written by God.

The conflict was too much for David; he ended up in a psychiatric hospital where he was told to join the OCD support group that I lead. He would not accept explanations from his family, friends or religious figures. His logic, fueled by his OCD, did not allow him any flexibility to reconcile the perceived conflict. He was taking medications to stay calm.

People who suffer from Religious Scrupulosity often obsess about the following:

God: do I do anything that could upset God? Prayer: am I praying correctly? Karma: I am a bad person, so something terrible will happen to me. Morality: I must always think pure thoughts. Sins: will I go to hell? Confession: I must tell someone everything on my mind that is inappropriate.

What to do and/or not do (Please read many times while obsessing and practice what is said):

These thoughts are not unique to you. They are universal to all people suffering from Religious Scrupulosity. Your OCD creates doubt, needs certainty and requires perfectionism. This type of thinking is normal to all people suffering from Obsessive Compulsive Disorder. Seeing these qualities of OCD will help you to overcome it.

People who suffer from Religious Scrupulosity OCD often suffer in silent agony. You think that you truly understand the issue at hand and that the whole world should think like you do. You use logic you have obtained from scriptures, spiritual teachers, priests, gurus, etc. You keep asking questions to reassure yourself only to ask more and more questions later. You may feel less anxious after some reassurance only to feel more anxious a few minutes later. You confess to clear your mind only to feel a need to confess again a few hours later.

Again, doubt and a need for certainty almost always accompany this type of OCD. You pray to neutralize your thoughts, but it takes a lot of your time and energy. Instead of feeling good about praying, you use it to avoid anxiety. You do all of these things not because you are a good religious person, but because you have OCD and experience a lot of anxiety and fear. Most people enjoy their religion; you spend most of the time obsessing about it. You have OCD.

You trust your OCD and do what it tells you to do which is to neutralize, confess, doubt and pray as methods of avoidance. You experience anxiety and confusion. You think and feel that it makes sense to do all of these things because you know the truth. But all you are doing is indulging your OCD.

Remember that you will experience anxiety, doubt and a need for certainty while working on your obsession and that it takes time to start feeling relief. As you start seeing your thoughts as an obsession and a product of your OCD, you will feel anxious. You will feel anxious because of your OCD. Do not give much credence to your feelings of anxiety. You are trying something new. Once you learn and practice how to handle Religious Scrupulosity, the anxiety will diminish.

Your life is limited because of OCD. Do not argue with your obsession. Do not try to reason with it. If you try to reason with it, it only gets stronger and more confusing to you. Understand that your mind has been giving you wrong information. It is time to stop validating these thoughts. You stop validating obsessions when you are no longer engaged in them. Not to engage with an obsession means not to have a conversation with it in your mind. As you argue with a thought or try to reassure yourself or agree with an obsession, you create an internal conflict.

This conflict must be eliminated for an obsession to pass. By not engaging with the obsession, you deprive it of the energy generated by the conflict and you allow the obsession to pass. When you engage your obsessions, you are back in the disorder.

In order not to engage an obsession, your attention has to be somewhere else. Your brain has a natural capacity to observe and be aware of thoughts. To be aware of your obsession means not to judge it or make conclusions about yourself or situations around you. To be aware is to be in a space free from thinking. To observe is not to think. It is as if thinking is happening, but judgment is not there. When you catch yourself judging, realize that judging is just another form of thinking.

To be aware is to create space for thoughts to arise, exist and dissipate. To be aware is to observe your emotions of fear and uncertainty and allow them to exist until they dissipate. To be aware is to step aside and let the obsession pass. To be aware is to learn to react less. To be aware is to see that an obsession, an image or an urge is just another thought or feeling. Thoughts and feelings pass if you let them be and do nothing about them. To be aware is to realize that not wanting to have an obsession or approaching it with aversion is to have more thoughts. To be aware is to let things be as they are. As you learn not to react to anxious thoughts, your nervous system gets stronger. In order for you to successfully manage your OCD, choose to connect to your awareness – it is a quiet and peaceful place and it is always there.

As you resist engaging in your Religious Obsessions, your anxiety and uncertainty increase. Remind yourself that you are suffering from OCD and therefore you are feeling these emotions. Do not argue with Religious Obsessions. Do not engage them. Let things be as they are. Stay in awareness, allow space for the feeling and obsessions to arise, exist and dissipate. It will make you stronger.

Summary:

Remember that your Religious Obsessions are not unique. All people suffering from Religious Scrupulosity think similar thoughts. You have

OCD and that is why you think and feel this way. Practice staying in awareness. Do not engage your obsessions. Let things be as they are. Do not validate your feelings or thoughts. Religious Obsessions may come every two minutes. Allow space for emotions and thoughts to arise, exist and dissipate.

SEXUAL OBSESSIONS

Irene is a lovely and kind twenty-year-old lady. She goes to college during the day and, for extra money, she used to babysit. She enjoys everything about kids. She plays with them, reads to them and goes to the park with them. You can see that one day she will make a great mother. But Irene no longer babysits as she worries that she will somehow sexually abuse the children by touching them inappropriately or even something worse.

Irene feels very depressed. Part of her knows that she would not abuse anyone and that she does not want to do that, but she is terrified because she has thoughts like this, and she cannot stop thinking these thoughts. She is afraid to be near children and thinks of herself as a pervert. Irene is deeply ashamed to share her fears with anyone as they may think that she actually wants to be inappropriate with children. Sometimes she thinks she should be in jail in order to keep others safe from her.

People who suffer from Sexual Obsession often think the following:

What if I touch myself sexually in front of somebody?
What if I want to touch a child sexually? I think of
having sex with my mother, father, brother or sister. I
have an urge to have sex with a child. I have an urge to
rape a woman. I have a lot of inappropriate sexual
thoughts and images. I can't stop thinking them — I must
like them.

**What to do and/or not do (Please read many
times while obsessing and practice what is
said):**

These thoughts are not unique to you. They are
universal to all people suffering from Sexual
Obsessions. Your OCD creates doubt, needs
certainty and requires perfectionism. This type of
thinking is normal to all people suffering from
Obsessive Compulsive Disorder. Seeing these
qualities of OCD will help you to overcome it.

People who suffer from Sexual Obsessions often
suffer in silent agony. You think you are the
worst person in the world. If people only knew
what you were thinking about, they would put
you in jail immediately. You think that because
you have these thoughts, you are a terrible person
and that deep inside you really want to do all of
these things. You determine who you are based

on these thoughts. You confess to clear your mind only to feel a need to confess again a few hours later. These thoughts keep coming, but you do not want to think them.

Again, doubt and a need for certainty almost always accompany this type of OCD. You want to know for sure that these are just thoughts and that it is not a big deal that you think them. But you think that you are a rotten person for having these thoughts. You resist them, you pray, you distrust your mind, you try to avoid them, but they keep coming back. You may even avoid being next to certain people. You do all of this because you have OCD and experience a lot of anxiety and fear. Research shows that many people have Sexual Thoughts, but they dismiss them right away. You cannot do that. You have OCD. You trust your OCD and you think terrible things about yourself. You experience anxiety and confusion. But all you are doing is indulging your OCD.

Remember that you will experience anxiety, doubt and a need for certainty while working on your disorder and that it takes time to start feeling relief. As you start seeing your thoughts as an obsession and a product of your OCD, you will feel anxious. You will feel anxious because of your OCD. Do not give much credence to your feelings of anxiety. You are trying something new. Once you learn and practice how to handle Sexual Obsessions, the anxiety will diminish.

Your life is limited because of OCD. Do not argue with your obsessions. Do not try to reason with them. If you try to reason with them, they only get stronger and more confusing to you. Understand that your mind has been giving you wrong information. It is time to stop validating these thoughts. You stop validating obsessions when you are no longer engaged in them. Not to engage with an obsession means not to have a conversation with it in your mind. As you argue with a thought or try to reassure yourself or agree with an obsession you create an internal conflict. This conflict must be eliminated for an obsession to pass. By not engaging with the obsession, you deprive it of the energy generated by the conflict and you allow the obsession to pass. When you engage your obsessions, you are back in the disorder.

In order not to engage an obsession, your attention has to be somewhere else. Your brain has a natural capacity to observe and be aware of thoughts. To be aware of your obsession means not to judge it or make conclusions about yourself or situations around you. To be aware is to be in a space free from thinking. To observe is not to think. It is as if thinking is happening, but judgment is not there. When you catch yourself judging, realize that judging is just another form of thinking.

To be aware is to create space for thoughts to arise, exist and dissipate. To be aware is to observe your emotions of fear and uncertainty and allow them to exist until they dissipate. To be aware is to step aside and let the obsession pass. To be aware is to learn to react less. To be aware is to see that an obsession, an image or an urge is just another thought or feeling. Thoughts and feelings pass if you let them be and do nothing about them. To be aware is to realize that not wanting to have an obsession or approaching it with aversion is to have more thoughts. To be aware is to let things be as they are. As you learn not to react to anxious thoughts, your nervous system gets stronger. In order for you to successfully manage your OCD, choose to connect to your awareness – it is a quiet and peaceful place and it is always there.

As you resist engaging your Sexual Obsessions, your anxiety and uncertainty will increase. Remind yourself that you are suffering from OCD and that is why you are feeling these emotions. Do not argue with Sexual Obsessions. Do not engage them. Let things be as they are. Stay in awareness, allow space for the feeling and obsessions to arise, exist and dissipate. It will make you stronger.

Summary:

Remember that your Sexual Obsessions are not unique. All people suffering from Sexual Obsessions think similar thoughts. You have OCD and that is why you think and feel this way. Practice staying in awareness. Do not engage your obsessions. Let things be as they are. Do not validate your feelings or thoughts. Sexual Obsessions may come every two minutes. Allow space for emotions and thoughts to arise, exist and dissipate. Do not avoid places or people.

VIOLENT OBSESSIONS

John has an MBA from a top university. He is very creative and intelligent. When he talks, you notice that he really knows what he is talking about. For fun, he taught himself IT development and now makes money working in business and doing IT. It seems there is nothing in the world he cannot do. But John is afraid to be in the same room or close to anyone that he determines to be weaker than he is.

He is afraid that he will lose control of himself and hurt someone. He often thinks violent and angry thoughts. He has never physically hurt anyone before, but he cannot stop thinking violent thoughts and visualizing violent images. And since he is thinking these thoughts, he assumes he is a violent and angry person. John does not come across as a violent and angry person; actually, he looks like a very nice person. All his friends think that he is a nice person. He cannot understand why he cannot stop thinking these thoughts.

People who suffer from Violent Obsessions often think the following:

If people knew what I am thinking, I would be in jail. I should just be in jail, because I am a danger to society. I could pick up a knife and kill my husband, wife, etc. I can hurt someone at any time. I will get angry and hurt someone. I feel like I have an urge to hurt someone, especially if I think they are weaker than I am. I am a terrible person for thinking these thoughts.

What to do and/or not do (Please read many times while obsessing and practice what is said):

These thoughts are not unique to you. They are universal to all people suffering from Violent Obsessions. Your OCD creates doubt, needs certainty and requires perfectionism. This type of thinking is normal to all people suffering from Obsessive Compulsive Disorder. Seeing these qualities of OCD will help you to overcome it.

People who suffer from Violent Obsessions often suffer in silent agony. You think you are the worst person in the world. If people only knew what you are thinking about, they would put you in jail immediately. You think that because you have these thoughts, you are a terrible person and that deep inside you really want to do all of these terrible things. You determine who you are based on these thoughts. You confess to others to clear your mind only to feel a need to confess again a few hours later. These thoughts keep coming up, but you do not want to think them.

Again, doubt and a need for certainty almost always accompany this type of OCD. You want to know for sure that these are just thoughts, that it is not a big deal that you think them and that you are not a terrible, out-of-control person. But you think that you are a rotten person for having these thoughts. You resist them, you pray, you distrust your mind, you try to avoid them, but they keep coming back. You may even avoid being near certain people. You do all of this because you have OCD and experience a lot of anxiety and fear. Research shows that many people have Violent Thoughts, but they have no problem dismissing them right away. You cannot do that. You have OCD. You trust your OCD and you think terrible things about yourself. You experience anxiety, shame and confusion. But all this does is to indulge your OCD.

Remember that you will experience anxiety, doubt and a need for certainty while working on your OCD and that it takes time to start feeling relief. As you start seeing your thoughts as an obsession and a product of your OCD, you will feel anxious. You will feel anxious because of your OCD. Do not give much credence to your feelings of anxiety. You are trying something new. Once you learn and practice how to handle Violent Obsessions, the anxiety will diminish.

Your life is limited because of OCD. Do not argue with your obsessions. Do not try to reason with them. If you try to reason with them, they only get stronger and more confusing. Understand that your mind has been giving you wrong information. It is time to stop validating these thoughts. You stop validating obsessions when you are no longer engaged in them. Not to engage with an obsession means not to have a conversation with it in your mind. As you argue with a thought or try to reassure yourself or agree with an obsession, you create an internal conflict. This conflict must be eliminated for an obsession to pass. By not engaging with the obsession, you deprive it of the energy generated by the conflict and you allow the obsession to pass. When you engage your obsessions, you are back in the disorder.

In order not to engage an obsession, your attention has to be somewhere else. Your brain has a natural capacity to observe and be aware of thoughts. To be aware of your obsessions means not to judge them or make conclusions about yourself or situations around you. To be aware is to be in a space free from thinking. To observe is not to think. It is as if thinking is happening, but judgment is not there. When you catch yourself judging, realize that judging is just another form of thinking.

To be aware is to create space for thoughts to arise, exist and dissipate. To be aware is to observe your emotions of fear and uncertainty and allow them to exist until they dissipate. To be aware is to step aside and let the obsession pass. To be aware is to learn to react less. To be aware is to see that an obsession, an image or an urge is just another thought or feeling. Thoughts and feelings pass if you let them be and do nothing about them. To be aware is to realize that not wanting to have an obsession or approaching it with aversion is to have more thoughts. To be aware is to let things be as they are. As you learn not to react to anxious thoughts, your nervous system gets stronger. In order for you to successfully manage your OCD, choose to connect to your awareness – it is a quiet and peaceful place and it is always there.

As you resist engaging your Violent Obsessions, your anxiety and uncertainty will increase. Remind yourself that you are suffering from OCD and that is why you are feeling these emotions. Do not argue with Violent Obsessions. Do not engage them. Let things be as they are. Stay in awareness, allow space for the feeling and obsessions to arise, exist and dissipate. It will make you stronger.

Summary:

Remember that your Violent Obsessions are not unique. All people suffering from Violent Obsessions think similar thoughts. You have OCD and that is why you think and feel this way. Practice staying in awareness. Do not engage your obsessions. Let things be as they are. Do not validate your feelings or thoughts. Violent Obsessions may come every two minutes. Allow space for emotions and thoughts to arise, exist and dissipate. Do not avoid places or people.

RESPONSIBILITY OCD

Jerry is a teacher in a public school. His students and coworkers like him. He looks forward to going to work every morning. It is only when he is teaching that he is not obsessing about being responsible for something.

Jerry does not want to watch the news or read newspapers anymore. For example, he hates when he hears that someone was killed while crossing a street. He immediately thinks he might have done it while driving a car and that he should go to a police precinct to report it. He feels responsible for things he imagined or thought. He does not think of himself as a person with high moral values, but he cannot stop obsessing about possible bad things he might have done.

People who suffer from Responsibility OCD often think the following:

If I notice something that can cause a problem to someone, I must fix it. If I have a thought about it, it would be my fault if I did not prevent it. I must always choose the best possible outcome. It is up to me to know what the right decision is. I have thought about it, so it is my fault. I must perform a perfect action or someone may get hurt.

What to do and/or not do (Please read many times while obsessing and practice what is said):

These thoughts are not unique to you. They are universal to all people suffering from Responsibility Obsessions. Your OCD creates doubt, needs certainty and requires perfectionism. This type of thinking is normal to all people suffering from Obsessive Compulsive Disorder. Seeing these qualities of OCD will help you to overcome it.

People who suffer from Responsibility Obsessions often suffer in many ways. You think you are the worst person in the world if you do not correct a situation. For example, you will spend hours cleaning a subway station to remove possible slip and fall hazards. Or, because you have thought about some horrible scenario and then heard about something like it in the news, it is your fault. Or you keep returning to a place where you were driving and hit a bump to make sure you didn't run anyone over. You think you must choose the best school for your child, because if something goes wrong with him or her you will spend the rest of your life in emotional pain. You give in to Responsibility Obsessions because the alternative for you is to suffer from guilt and shame and to feel a lot of anxiety.

Responsibility OCD is based on doubt, uncertainty, perfectionism and fear. When you obsess, you feel so many different emotions that you think your mind is trying to help you to become a better person or to save someone from possible troubles. In reality, you have OCD and that is why you are having these thoughts and feelings. You trust your OCD too much. You experience anxiety, shame and confusion. But all you're doing is indulging your OCD.

Remember that you will experience anxiety, doubt and a need for certainty while working on your OCD and that it takes time to start feeling relief. As you start seeing your Responsibility thoughts as an obsession and a product of your OCD, you will feel anxious. You will feel anxious because of your OCD. Do not give much credence to your feelings of anxiety. You are trying something new. Once you learn and practice how to handle Responsibility

Obsessions, the anxiety will diminish.

Your life is limited because of OCD. Do not argue with your obsessions. Do not try to reason with them. If you try to reason with them, they only get stronger and more confusing to you. See that your mind has been giving you wrong information. It is time to stop validating these thoughts. You stop validating obsessions when you are no longer engaged in them. Not to engage with an obsession means not to have a conversation with it in your mind. As you argue with a thought or try to reassure yourself or agree with an obsession, you create an internal conflict. This conflict must be eliminated for an obsession to pass. By not engaging with the obsession, you deprive it of the energy generated by the conflict and you allow the obsession to pass. When you engage your obsessions, you are back in the disorder.

In order not to engage an obsession, your attention has to be somewhere else. Your brain has a natural capacity to observe and be aware of thoughts. To be aware of your obsessions means not to judge them or make conclusions about yourself or situations around you. To be aware is to be in a space free from thinking. To observe is not to think. It is as if thinking is happening, but judgment is not there. When you catch yourself judging, realize that judging is just another form of thinking.

To be aware is to create space for thoughts to arise, exist and dissipate. To be aware is to observe your emotions of fear and uncertainty and allow them to exist until they dissipate. To be aware is to step aside and let the obsession pass. To be aware is to learn to react less. To be aware is to see that an obsession, an image or an urge is just another thought or feeling. Thoughts and feelings pass if you let them be and do nothing about them. To be aware is to realize that not wanting to have an obsession or approaching it with aversion is to have more thoughts. To be aware is to let things be as they are. As you learn not to react to anxious thoughts, your nervous system gets stronger. In order for you to successfully manage your OCD, choose to connect to your awareness – it is a quiet and peaceful place and it is always there.

As you resist engaging your Responsibility Obsessions, your anxiety, doubt and uncertainty will increase. Remind yourself that you are suffering from OCD and that is why you are feeling these emotions. Do not argue with Responsibility Obsessions. Do not engage them. Let things be as they are. Stay in awareness, allow space for the feeling and obsessions to arise, exist and dissipate. It will make you stronger.

Summary:

Remember your Responsibility Obsessions are not unique. All people suffering from Responsibility OCD think similar thoughts. You have OCD and that is why you think and feel this way. Practice staying in awareness. Do not engage your obsessions. Let things be as they are. Do not validate your feelings or thoughts. Responsibility Obsessions may come every two minutes. Allow space for emotions and thoughts to arise, exist and dissipate. Do not avoid places or people. Take a few minutes of doing nothing to allow the emotion to dissipate.

CONTROLLING "BAD" THOUGHTS

Henry tries to be a good person. In fact, he is a good person. He is sincere and kind. He helps his family financially and emotionally. They rely on him for support. They know they can call him any time for advice. Henry has a good job and he reads a lot of philosophy and religion. He is not very religious, but calls himself spiritual. Henry struggles with having "bad" thoughts.

Henry understands that he is a decent person, but he gets very tough on himself for having angry, jealous and/or hateful thoughts. He keeps thinking that a good person would not have these thoughts, but he cannot help himself. He does not want to think these thoughts, but as he tries not to, he thinks them more. This is very frustrating for him. Not only does he not want to think them, he believes these thoughts create bad energy, bad karma and damage the environment around him. Henry thinks that he should be able to control his "bad" thoughts, or not have them in the first place. He constantly thinks about what is wrong with him.

People who suffer from Intrusive or Inappropriate Obsessions often think the following:

I should not be thinking this thought. It is a bad thought and because I am thinking it, I must be a bad person. I hate some of my thoughts. I can't stop thinking them and my thoughts are very disturbing to me. I must avoid having these thoughts.

What to do and/or not do (Please read many times while obsessing and practice what is said):

These thoughts are not unique to you. They are universal to all people suffering from Intrusive or Inappropriate Obsessions. Your OCD creates fear and anxiety, but this type of thinking is normal to all people suffering from Obsessive Compulsive Disorder.

People who suffer from Intrusive or Inappropriate Obsessions often suffer in silent agony. You spend a lot of your time trying to avoid these thoughts. You think that because you have these thoughts, that you are a terrible person. You determine who you are based on these thoughts. You hate them, yet they do not go away. These thoughts keep coming up, but you do not want to think them.

Again, doubt and a need for certainty almost always accompany this type of OCD. You want to know for sure that these are just thoughts, that it is not a big deal that you think them and that you are not a terrible, out-of-control person. But you think that you are a rotten person for having these thoughts. You resist them, you pray, you distrust your mind, you try to avoid them, but they keep coming back. In fact, the more you try to avoid the thoughts, the stronger they tend to get. You do all of this because you have OCD and experience a lot of anxiety and fear. You trust your OCD and you think terrible things about yourself. You experience anxiety, shame and confusion. But all you are doing is indulging your OCD.

Remember that you will experience anxiety, doubt and a need for certainty while working on your OCD and that it takes time to start feeling relief. As you start seeing your thoughts as an obsession and a product of your OCD, you will feel anxious. You will feel anxious because of your OCD. Do not give much credence to your feelings of anxiety. You are trying something new. Once you learn and practice how to handle Intrusive or Inappropriate Obsessions, the anxiety will diminish.

Your life is limited because of OCD. Do not argue with your obsessions. Do not try to reason with them. If you try to reason with them, they only get stronger and more confusing. Understand that your mind has been giving you wrong information. It is time to stop validating these thoughts. You stop validating obsessions when you are no longer engaged in them. Not to engage with an obsession means not to have a conversation with it in your mind. As you argue with a thought or try to reassure yourself or agree with an obsession, you create an internal conflict. This conflict must be eliminated for an obsession to pass. By not engaging with the obsession, you deprive it of the energy generated by the conflict and you allow the obsession to pass. When you engage your obsessions, you are back in the disorder.

In order not to engage an obsession, your attention has to be somewhere else. Your brain has a natural capacity to observe and be aware of thoughts. To be aware of your obsessions means not to judge them or make conclusions about yourself or situations around you. To be aware is to be in a space free from thinking. To observe is not to think. It is as if thinking is happening, but judgment is not there. When you catch yourself judging, realize that judging is just another form of thinking.

To be aware is to create space for thoughts to arise, exist and dissipate. To be aware is to observe your emotions of fear and uncertainty and allow them to exist until they dissipate. To be aware is to step aside and let the obsession pass. To be aware is to learn to react less. To be aware is to see that an obsession, an image or an urge is just another thought or feeling. Thoughts and feelings pass if you let them be and do nothing about them. To be aware is to realize that not wanting to have an obsession or approaching it with aversion is to have more thoughts. To be aware is to let things be as they are. As you learn not to react to anxious thoughts, your nervous system gets stronger. In order for you to successfully manage your OCD, choose to connect to your awareness – it is a quiet and peaceful place and it is always there.

As you resist engaging your Intrusive or Inappropriate Obsessions, your anxiety and uncertainty will increase. Remind yourself that you are suffering from OCD and that is why you are feeling these emotions. Do not argue with Intrusive or Inappropriate Obsessions. Do not engage them. Let things be as they are. Stay in awareness, allow space for the feeling and obsessions to arise, exist and dissipate. It will make you stronger.

Summary:

Remember that your Intrusive or Inappropriate Obsessions are not unique. All people suffering from Intrusive or Inappropriate Obsessions think similar thoughts. You have OCD and that is why you think and feel this way. Practice staying in awareness. Do not engage your obsessions. Let things be as they are. Do not validate your feelings or thoughts. Intrusive or Inappropriate Obsessions may come every two minutes. Allow space for emotions and thoughts to arise, exist and dissipate. Do not avoid places or people and remember that the more you do not want to have these thoughts the more they are going to stay.

HEALTH ANXIETY

Lisa works for a major financial company. She is great at her job and especially proud of her organizational skills. She is well-respected and well-liked at work.

Lisa thinks about cancer all the time. One year she had over 80 MRIs. It is hard to believe that an insurance company would continue paying for her tests, but they seem to do so. She visits a number of different doctors to get MRI referrals. Lisa does not tell them how many MRIs she's had or how often she gets tested. Sometimes she brings the results to my office and asks me to help her comprehend what they say. Her brain does not register anymore that the results are negative and there is nothing wrong with her.

People who suffer from Health Related Obsessions worry about their health:

What if I have cancer? What if I am having a heart attack, a stroke? There is something wrong with my eyes, prostate gland, mouth, etc. If I swallow this pill, I will choke. If I eat a slice of pizza, I will have high cholesterol. If I have a glass of wine, I will develop liver problems. This medication will give me terrible side effects.

*My father, mother, etc. died from a heart attack and
therefore I will also die from one.*

**What to do and/or not do (Please read many
times while obsessing and practice what is
said):**

Your OCD creates doubt, a need for certainty
and anxiety. This type of thinking is normal to all
people suffering from Obsessive Compulsive
Disorder. Seeing these qualities of OCD will
help you to overcome it.

It makes sense to be concerned about your
health. Your loved ones will encourage you to go
and get your symptoms checked out. You go to
a doctor for reassurance, only to be back in the
doctor's office few days later. You have many
MRIs, checkups and examinations, but you still
feel there could be something wrong with you.
Every cold, every physical sensation, every
discomfort is a possible catastrophic illness that
may kill you. Part of you knows that you are
experiencing anxiety, but another part (the OCD)
keeps telling you to check it out just in case, or
that you have a special reason to do so. You
see/hear/read about many people dying from
various diseases and you do not want to be

arrogant about your health so you check it out. Again. But it is never enough. The Health Anxiety monster wants more reassurance, more comfort.

Even your doctors tell you to stop asking so many questions and not to worry, but you can't stop. It is your health after all. Again, doubt and a need for certainty almost always accompany this type of OCD. You want to know for sure that you are not sick, but after a while you can't even hear the doctors' answers. You want to stop worrying about your health, but you cannot do that. You have OCD. You trust your OCD and you keep performing the rituals of going to doctors for reassurance. You experience anxiety, shame and confusion. But all you are doing is indulging your OCD.

Remember that you will experience anxiety, doubt and a need for certainty while working on your OCD and that it takes time to start feeling relief. As you start seeing your thoughts as an obsession and a product of your OCD, you will feel anxious. You will feel anxious because of your OCD. Do not give much credence to your feelings of anxiety. You are trying something

new. Once you learn and practice how to handle
Health Obsessions, the anxiety will diminish.

Your life is limited because of OCD. Do not
argue with your obsessions. Do not try to reason
with them. If you try to reason with them, they
only get stronger and more confusing to you.
Understand that your mind has been giving you
wrong information. It is time to stop validating
these thoughts. You stop validating obsessions
when you are no longer engaged in them. Not to
engage with an obsession means not to have a
conversation with it in your mind. As you argue
with a thought or try to reassure yourself or agree
with an obsession, you create an internal conflict.
This conflict must be eliminated for an obsession
to pass. By not engaging with the obsession, you
deprive it of the energy generated by the conflict
and you allow the obsession to pass. When you
engage your obsessions, you are back in the
disorder.

In order not to engage an obsession, your
attention has to be somewhere else. Your brain
has a natural capacity to observe and be aware of
thoughts. To be aware of your obsessions means
not to judge them or make conclusions about

yourself or situations around you. To be aware is to be in a space free from thinking. To observe is not to think. It is as if thinking is happening, but judgment is not there. When you catch yourself judging, realize that judging is just another form of thinking.

To be aware is to create space for thoughts to arise, exist and dissipate. To be aware is to observe your emotions of fear and uncertainty and allow them to exist until they dissipate. To be aware is to step aside and let the obsession pass. To be aware is to learn to react less. To be aware is to see that an obsession, an image or an urge is just another thought or feeling. Thoughts and feelings pass if you let them be and do nothing about them. To be aware is to realize that not wanting to have an obsession or approaching it with aversion is to have more thoughts. To be aware is to let things be as they are. As you learn not to react to anxious thoughts, your nervous system gets stronger. In order for you to successfully manage your OCD, choose to connect to your awareness – it is a quiet and peaceful place and it is always there.

As you resist engaging your Health Obsessions,

your anxiety and uncertainty will increase. Remind yourself that you are suffering from OCD and that is why you are constantly having urges to go to doctors. Do not argue with Health Obsessions. Do not engage them. Let things be as they are. Stay in awareness, allow space for the feeling and obsessions to arise, exist and dissipate. It will make you stronger.

Summary:

Remember that your Health Obsessions are not unique. All people suffering from Health Obsessions think similar thoughts. You have OCD and that is why you think and feel this way. Practice staying in awareness. Do not engage your obsessions. Let things be as they are. Do not validate your feelings or thoughts. Health Obsessions may come every two minutes. Allow space for emotions and thoughts to arise, exist and dissipate. As you practice not engaging with your Health Obsessions, resist calling doctors right away. Wait a day or two. When you see a doctor, simply explain what you are feeling and ask him or her if there is a problem. Let the doctors do the tests and then let you know if anything more needs to be done. No more questions. You can't afford to continue asking too many questions or researching on the Internet. The health anxiety OCD is a very strong illness – too many questions or Internet searches are not beneficial in this case.

BODY OBSESSIONS

Michael is a counselor working for a major non-profit organization. He makes a living giving advice to others. He helps clients deal with jobs, family matters and emotional issues. He is a likable and handsome man.

He thinks that his hair is receding and that he looks like a freak. Because of this belief, Michel's outlook on his future is very bleak. He thinks he will not be able to get married, he feels very insecure and he constantly checks to see if anyone is staring at his hair. He often has suicidal thoughts.

People who suffer from Body Obsessions often think the following:

My hair looks like it is receding. My nose is too big. My belly is disgustingly fat. My ankles are ugly. My skin looks terrible. I look like a freak. I look unnatural.

What to do and/or not do (Please read many times while obsessing and practice what is said):

These thoughts are not unique to you. They are universal to all people suffering from Body Obsessions. Your OCD creates anxiety and requires perfectionism. This type of thinking is normal to all people suffering from Obsessive Compulsive Disorder. Seeing these qualities of OCD will help you to overcome it.

People who suffer from Body Obsessions often experience a lot of shame and anxiety. You think that you are unattractive, a freakish looking person. You think everybody notices your body's defects. You stare at your body in the mirror noticing every little problem. You spend hours applying makeup on yourself. You cover your body. You compare yourself with others. You feel disgusted with yourself.

Again, doubt and a need for certainty almost always accompany this type of OCD. You want to know for sure that you do not look like a freak. You want to know that others are not judging you and you keep obsessing. You keep obsessing because you have OCD. You cannot stop because of it. There will always be some kind of reason to obsess about your body. How much can you take? When will it stop? You trust your OCD and it gives you shame, anxiety and fear. All you do is indulge your OCD.

Remember that you will experience anxiety, doubt and a need for certainty while working on your OCD and that it takes time to start feeling relief. As you start seeing your thoughts as an obsession and a product of your OCD, you will feel anxious. You will feel anxious because of your OCD. Do not give much credence to your feelings of anxiety. You are trying something new. Once you learn and practice how to handle Body Obsessions, the anxiety will diminish.

Your life is limited because of OCD. Do not argue with your obsessions. Do not try to reason with them. If you try to reason with them, they only get stronger and more confusing to you. Understand that your mind has been giving you wrong information. It is time to stop validating these thoughts. You stop validating obsessions when you are no longer engaged in them. Not to engage with an obsession means not to have a conversation with it in your mind. As you argue with a thought or try to reassure yourself or agree with an obsession, you create an internal conflict. This conflict must be eliminated for an obsession to pass. By not engaging with the obsession, you deprive it of the energy generated by the conflict and you allow the obsession to pass. When you engage your obsessions, you are back in the disorder.

In order not to engage an obsession, your attention has to be somewhere else. Your brain has a natural capacity to observe and be aware of the thoughts. To be aware of your obsessions means not to judge them or make conclusions about yourself or situations around you. To be aware is to be in a space free from thinking. To observe is not to think. It is as if thinking is happening, but judgment is not there. When you catch yourself judging, realize that judging is just another form of thinking.

To be aware is to create space for thoughts to arise, exist and dissipate. To be aware is to observe your emotions of fear and uncertainty and allow them to exist until they dissipate. To be aware is to step aside and let the obsession pass. To be aware is to learn to react less. To be aware is to see that an obsession, an image or an urge is just another thought or feeling. Thoughts and feelings pass if you let them be and do nothing about them. To be aware is to realize that not wanting to have an obsession or approaching it with aversion is to have more thoughts. To be aware is to let things be as they are. As you learn not to react to anxious thoughts, your nervous system gets stronger. In order for you to successfully manage your OCD, choose to connect to your awareness – it is a quiet and peaceful place and it is always there.

As you resist engaging your Body Obsessions, your anxiety and uncertainty will increase. Remind yourself that you are suffering from OCD and that is why you are feeling these emotions. Do not argue with Body Obsessions. Do not engage them. Let things be as they are. Stay in awareness, allow space for the feeling and obsessions to arise, exist and dissipate. It will make you stronger.

Summary:

Remember that your Body Obsessions are not unique. All people suffering from Body Obsessions think similar thoughts. You have OCD and that is why you think and feel this way. Practice staying in awareness. Do not engage your obsessions. Let things be as they are. Do not validate your feelings or thoughts. Body Obsessions may come every two minutes. Allow space for emotions and thoughts to arise, exist and dissipate. Do not avoid places or people. It is OK to walk away from the mirror without feeling completely good about your looks. Give yourself a few minutes to feel anxiety and/or shame. These feelings will diminish if you let them be. Do not ask for reassurance that you look OK.

PANIC ATTACKS

People who suffer from OCD sometimes will have a Panic Attack. For some people, the stress of having Panic Attacks makes OCD more prominent. After having a few Panic Attacks, you begin to feel out of control. You try to resist and be strong, but it seems to make you feel more out of control. You begin to think that you may die, make a fool out of yourself, that no one cares about you, or that you are going crazy. You may even start avoiding places or people. You may feel desperate, frustrated and sad.

What to do and/or not do (Please read many times while obsessing and practice what is said):

It seems that Panic Attacks and Obsessive Thinking are related. People may have Panic Attacks because of Obsessive Thinking and Panic Attacks may make OCD worse. You do not have to stop working on your OCD in order to take care of your Panic Attacks. As you work with your Obsessive Thinking, you can apply similar concepts to your Panic Attacks.

Think of your Panic Attack as a release of

excessive nervous energy. As you get anxious,
the energy has to move somewhere. Do not
resist it. Let it move freely through the body.
You do not have to like or dislike the sensations
you are feeling inside. Keep the body relaxed.
Think your body has no muscles. No resistance.
Stay away from engaging your thoughts. Do not
try to calm yourself down. Know that you are
having a Panic Attack, that you have had them
before and have survived them. Be in awareness
and let everything be as it is.

Awareness is a place where a thought is not the
most important thing in your brain. Sometimes
your anxiety will get higher before it gets lower –
this is normal. Let the fear be and do nothing
about it. Do not push it away, do not validate it,
do not create false conclusions about what may
be happening or what your life may become.
Stay in awareness and do not engage your scary
thoughts or give yourself empty reassurances.

To be aware is to create space for thoughts to
arise, exist and dissipate. To be aware is to
observe your fear and anxiety and allow them to
exist until they dissipate. To be aware is to step
aside and let the obsession pass. To be aware is

to learn to react less. To be aware is to see that an obsession, an image or an urge is just another thought or a feeling. Thoughts and feelings pass if you let them be and do nothing about them. To be aware is to realize that not wanting to have an obsession or approaching it with aversion is to have more thoughts. To be aware is to let things be as they are. As you learn not to react to anxious thoughts, your nervous system gets stronger. In order for you to successfully manage your Panic Attacks, choose to connect to your awareness – it is a quiet and peaceful place and it is always there.

Summary:

Dealing successfully with Panic Attacks requires knowledge of what not to do. Do not fight them, do not hate them or fear them. When having a Panic Attack, relax your body, have no resistance. Know that you are having a Panic Attack, stay in awareness, and do not think with the anxiety and fear you are feeling. Think of a Panic Attack as a release of excessive nervous energy. Do not avoid people or places.

DEPRESSION

Depression often accompanies OCD. It is understandable that from a psychological point of view, you would feel sad or depressed that you cannot stop obsessing. Bleak thoughts about your current situation and your future may come often and may result in depression. You may think that nothing will ever change. You believe you have a mental illness and that there is nothing you can do to stop it. Your mind is out of control. You end up feeling depressed and thinking depressive thoughts.

What to do and/or not do (Please read many times while feeling depressed and practice what is said):

These thoughts are common to people with depression. You think that your present and your future are bad. You feel downhearted and heavy. You think you are helpless and sick. Seeing these thoughts as symptoms of Depression will help you to overcome them. Depression can be scary but, just like OCD, you can manage it and get better.

As you work on your OCD, you may start feeling

more positive, more in control. Two things are very important to overcome your Depression: detach from your thoughts and stay in awareness. Awareness is the place where thoughts are not the most important things. To detach from depressive thoughts and feelings is to see them as symptoms of Depression and not as your reality. It is very important not to validate them or engage them. Do not push them away. A feeling of Depression, no matter how unpleasant it is, must be felt fully. Lose the resistance to the feeling. Abandon the resistance to the thoughts. Know that your awareness is free from thoughts.

While you are changing your relationship with Depression, familiarize yourself with awareness. Do not argue with your depressive thoughts. Do not try to reason with them. If you try to reason with them, they only get stronger and more confusing to you. Not to engage with depressive thoughts means not to have a conversation with it in your mind. As you argue with a thought or try to reassure yourself or agree with it, you create an internal conflict. This conflict must be eliminated for a depressive thought and feeling to pass. By not engaging with the thought or feeling, you deprive it of the energy generated by

the conflict and you allow the depression to pass.
When you engage your depressive thoughts, you
are back in the disorder.

Your brain has a natural capacity to observe and
be aware of thoughts. To be aware of your
Depressive Thoughts means not to judge them or
make conclusions about yourself or situations
around you. To be aware is to be in a space free
from thinking. To observe is not to think. It is
as if thinking is happening, but judgment is not
there. When you catch yourself judging, realize
that judging is just another form of thinking.

To be aware is to create space for thoughts to
arise, exist and dissipate. To be aware is to
observe your emotions of fear and uncertainty
and allow them to exist until they dissipate. To
be aware is to step aside and let the obsession
pass. To be aware is to learn to react less. To be
aware is to see that an obsession, an image or an
urge is just another thought or feeling. Thoughts
and feelings pass if you let them be and do
nothing about them. To be aware is to realize
that not wanting to have depressive thought or
approaching it with aversion is to have more
thoughts. To be aware is to let things be as they

are. In order for you to successfully manage your Depression, choose to connect to your awareness – it is a quiet and peaceful place and it is always there.

Summary:

Remember that your Depressive Thoughts and feelings are not unique. All people suffering from Depression think similar thoughts. As you fully accept Depressive Thoughts and feelings, practice staying in awareness. Do not engage your Depressive Thoughts. Let things be as they are. Do not validate your feelings or thoughts. Depressive Thoughts and feelings may come every two minutes. Allow space for emotions and thoughts to arise, exist and dissipate. Do not avoid places or people. Keep your schedule of daily activities.

ABOUT THE AUTHOR

Boris Pisman is a New York state-licensed mental health counselor in private practice. He worked as a therapist at White Plains Hospital – Behavioral Health specializing in OCD and anxiety. The Behavioral Therapy Institute certified Boris in Exposure and Response Prevention Treatment. For most of his adult life, Boris has practiced and taught yoga, meditation and non-dualistic philosophy in the United States and India.

Printed in Great Britain
by Amazon.co.uk, Ltd.,
Marston Gate.